HAL·LEONARD
UKULELE PLAY-ALONG

AUDIO ACCESS INCLUDED

VOL. 29

Over the Rainbow
& Other Favorites

Play 8 of Your Favorite Songs with Professional Audio Tracks

PLAYBACK+
Speed • Pitch • Balance • Loop

To access audio visit:
www.halleonard.com/mylibrary

Enter Code
3408-5355-5330-9086

Ukulele by Chris Kringel

ISBN 978-1-4803-3043-6

HAL·LEONARD®

Visit Hal Leonard Online at
www.halleonard.com

Contact us:
Hal Leonard
7777 West Bluemound Road
Milwaukee, WI 53213
Email: info@halleonard.com

In Europe, contact:
Hal Leonard Europe Limited
42 Wigmore Street
Marylebone, London, W1U 2RN
Email: info@halleonardeurope.com

In Australia, contact:
Hal Leonard Australia Pty. Ltd.
4 Lentara Court
Cheltenham, Victoria, 3192 Australia
Email: info@halleonard.com.au

Bring Me Sunshine

Words by Sylvia Dee
Music by Arthur Kent

First note

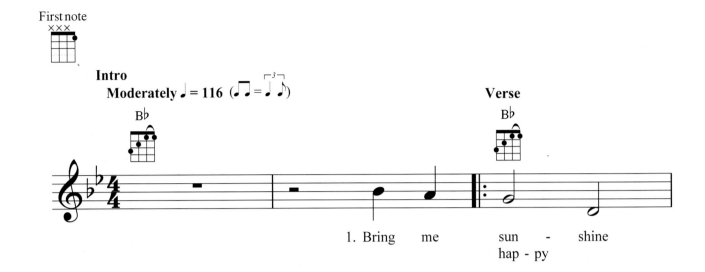

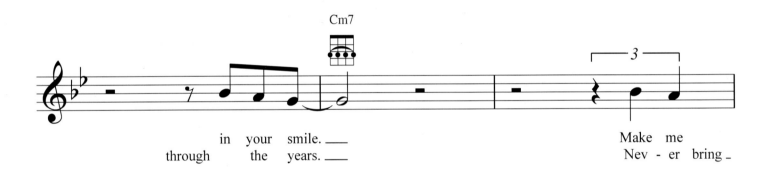

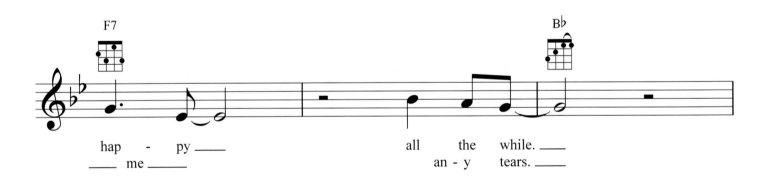

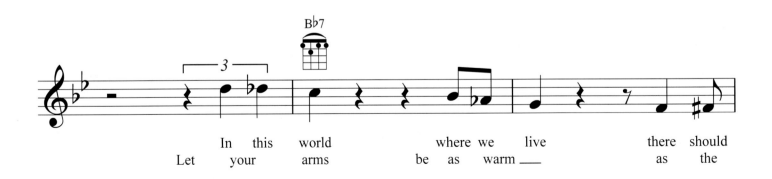

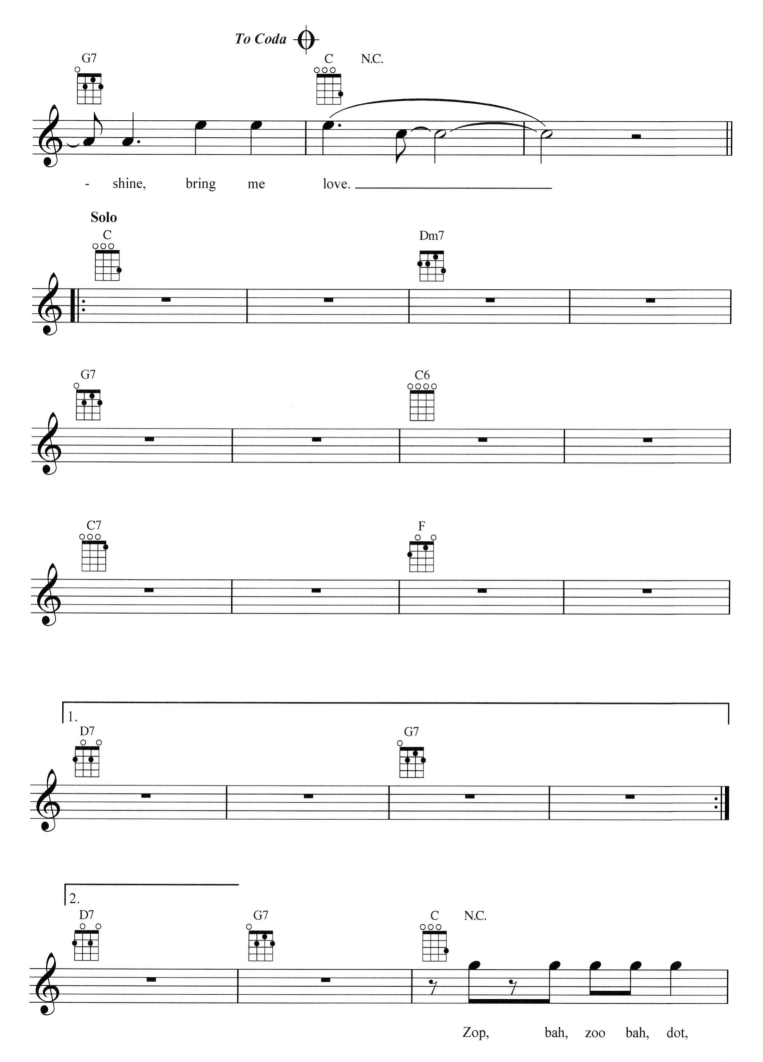

Mr. Bojangles

Words and Music by Jerry Jeff Walker

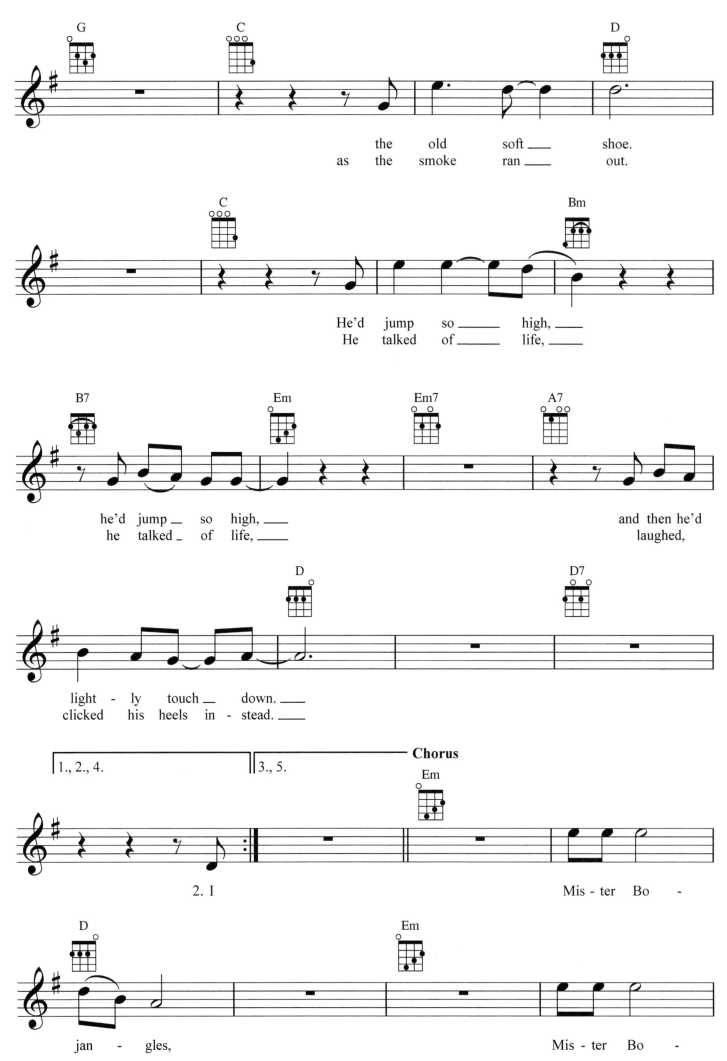

the old soft ____ shoe.
as the smoke ran ____ out.

He'd jump so ____ high, ____
He talked of ____ life, ____

he'd jump ___ so high, ____
he talked ___ of life, ____

and then he'd
laughed,

light - ly touch ___ down. ____
clicked his heels in - stead. ____

1., 2., 4.

3., 5.

Chorus

2. I

Mis - ter Bo -

jan - gles,

Mis - ter Bo -

8

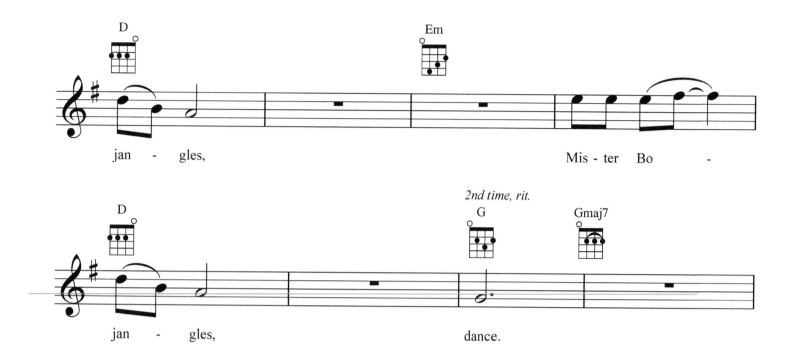

jan - gles,   Mis - ter   Bo   -

jan - gles,   dance.

4. He

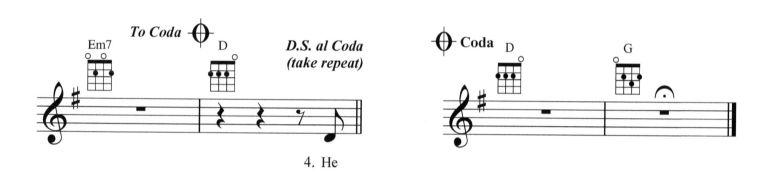

Additional Lyrics

3. He said his name, Bojangles, and he danced a lick across the cell.
   He grabbed his pants in feathered stance 'fore he jumped so high,
   And then he clicked his heels.
   He let go a laugh, he let go a laugh,
   Shook back his clothes all around.

4. He danced for those at minstrel shows and county fairs throughout the south.
   He spoke with tears of fifteen years, how his dog and him traveled about.
   The dog up and died, he up and died.
   After twenty years, he still grieves.

5. He said, "I dance now at ev'ry chance in honky-tonks for drinks and tips.
   But most the time I spend behind these county bars 'cause I drinks a bit."
   He shook his head, and as he shook his head,
   I heard someone ask him: Please, please...

Escape

(The Piña Colada Song)

Words and Music by Rupert Holmes

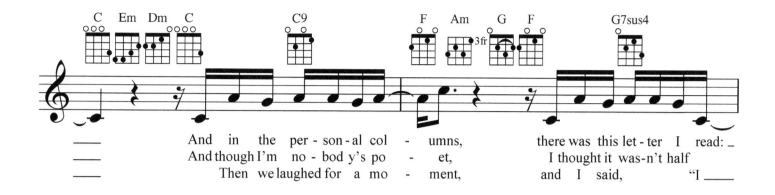

—— And in the per - son - al col - umns, there was this let - ter I read: _
—— And though I'm no - bod y's po - et, I thought it was-n't half
—— Then we laughed for a mo - ment, and I said, "I ——

Chorus

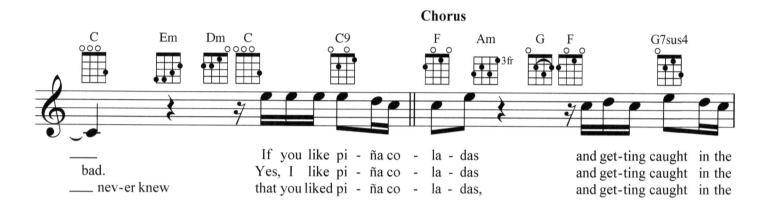

—— bad.
—— nev-er knew
If you like pi - ña co - la - das
Yes, I like pi - ña co - la - das
that you liked pi - ña co - la - das,
and get-ting caught in the
and get-ting caught in the
and get-ting caught in the

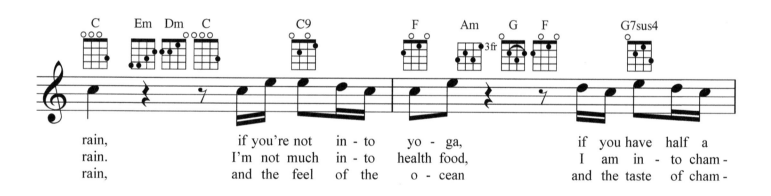

rain,
rain.
rain,
if you're not in - to yo - ga,
I'm not much in - to health food,
and the feel of the o - cean
if you have half a
I am in - to cham -
and the taste of cham -

brain,
pagne.
pagne.
if you like mak-ing love at mid - night
I've got to meet you by to - mor-row noon,
If you like mak-ing love at mid - night
in the dunes
and cut through all this red
in the dunes

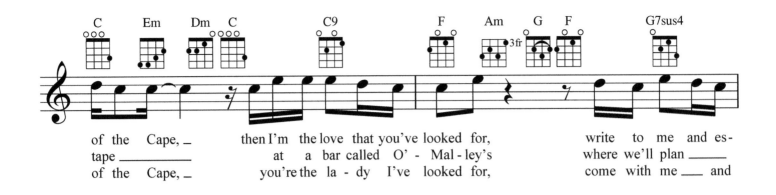

of the Cape, _   then I'm the love that you've looked for,   write to me and es-
tape _____   at a bar called O' - Mal - ley's   where we'll plan _____
of the Cape, _   you're the la - dy I've looked for,   come with me ___ and

Interlude

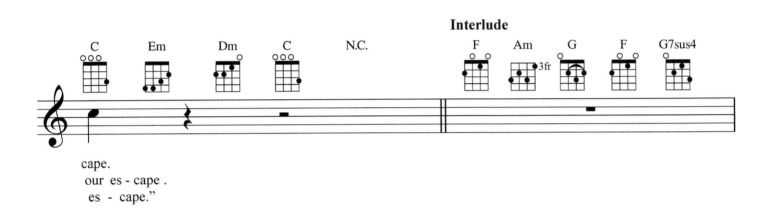

cape.
our es - cape .
es - cape."

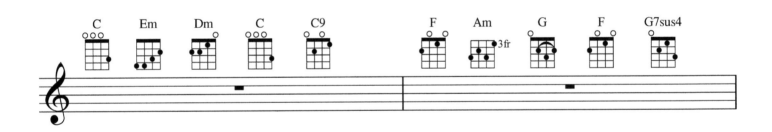

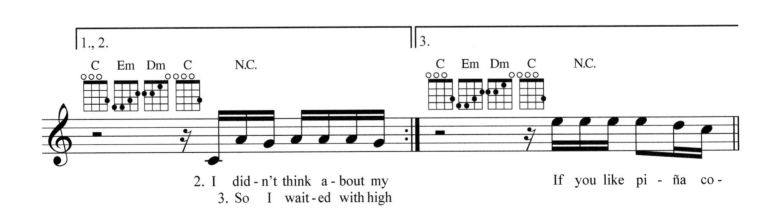

2. I did - n't think a - bout my
3. So I wait - ed with high

If you like pi - ña co -

Outro-Chorus

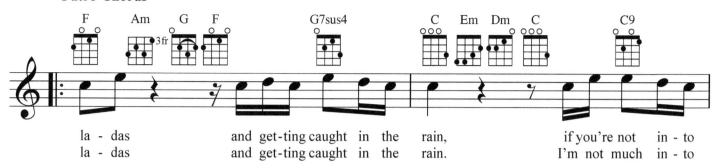

la - das   and get-ting caught in the   rain,   if you're not   in - to
la - das   and get-ting caught in the   rain.   I'm not much   in - to

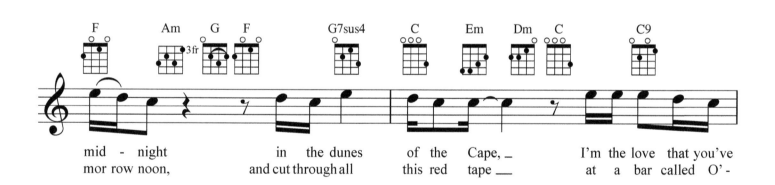

yo - ga,   if you have half a   brain,   if you like mak - ing love at
health food,   I am in - to cham - pagne.   I've got to meet you by to -

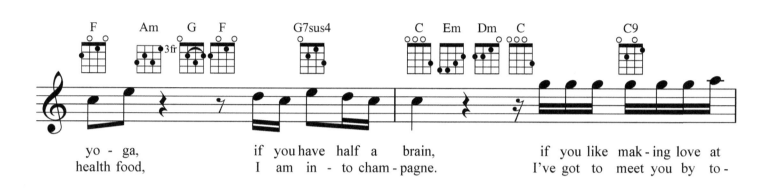

mid - night   in the dunes   of the   Cape, _   I'm the love that you've
mor row noon,   and cut through all   this red   tape __   at a bar called O' -

Repeat and fade

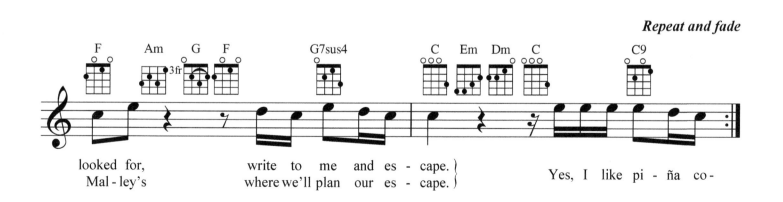

looked for,   write to me and es - cape. ⎱
Mal - ley's   where we'll plan our es - cape. ⎰   Yes, I like pi - ña co -

Good Morning Starshine

from the Broadway Musical Production HAIR
Words by James Rado and Gerome Ragni
Music by Galt MacDermot

First note

Intro
Moderately ♩ = 124

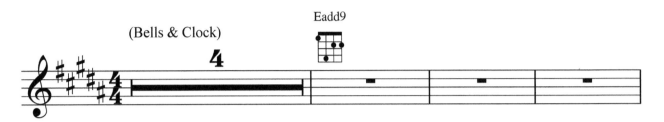

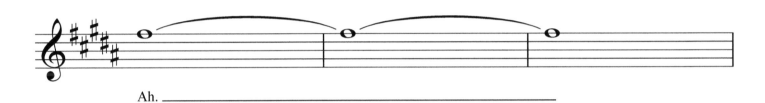

Ah. _____

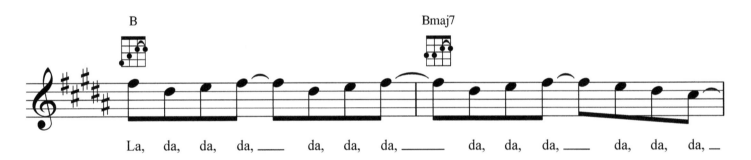

La, da, da, da, _____ da, da, da, _____ da, da, da, _____ da, da, da, _

_____ da, da, la, _____ la.

La, da, da, da, ____ da, da, da, ____ da, dom, ___ da, da,

Happy Together

Words and Music by Garry Bonner and Alan Gordon

geth - er. _____ 2. If I should geth - er. _____

Chorus

I can't see me

lov - ing no - bod - y but you for all my life. ___

When you're with me,

ba - by the skies ___ will be blue for all my life. ___

𝄋 **Verse**

_____ 3., 4., 5. Me and you and you and

ba, _____ ba, ba. Ba, ba, ba, ba,

⊕ Coda
Outro

D.S. al Coda

ba.) _____ geth - er. _____

___ So hap - py to - geth - er. _____ And how is the

weath - er? _____ So hap - py to - geth - er. _____

___ We're hap - py to - geth - er. _____

Play 4 times

___ So hap - py to - geth - er. _____

Let the Sunshine In

from the Broadway Musical Production HAIR
Words by James Rado and Gerome Ragni
Music by Galt MacDermot

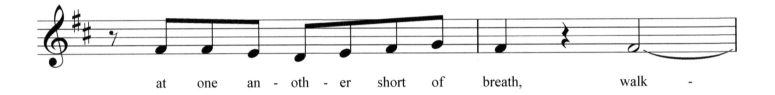

at one an - oth - er short of breath, walk -

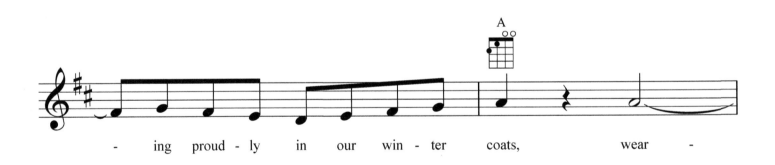

- ing proud - ly in our win - ter coats, wear -

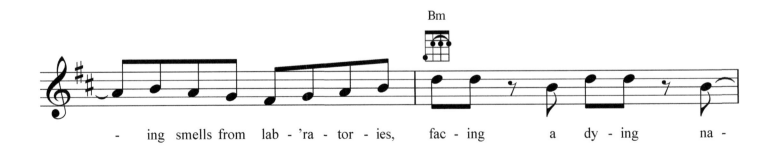

- ing smells from lab - 'ra - tor - ies, fac - ing a dy - ing na -

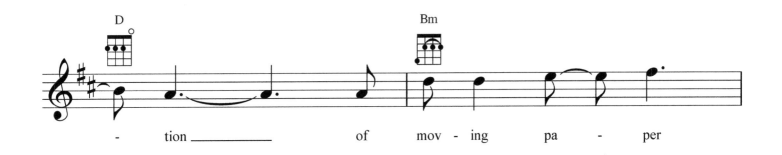

- tion _____ of mov - ing pa - per

fan - ta - sy. Lis - t'ning for the new - told lies ___

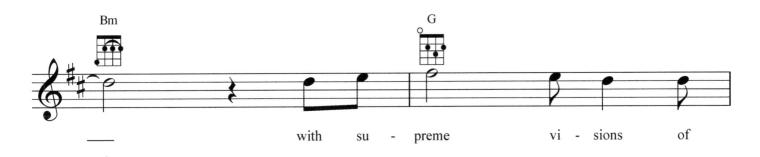

___ with su - preme vi - sions of

To Coda ⊕

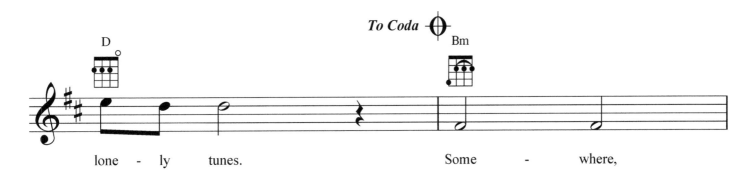

lone - ly tunes. Some - where,

in - side some - thing, there is a rush of

great - ness. Who knows what stands in front of

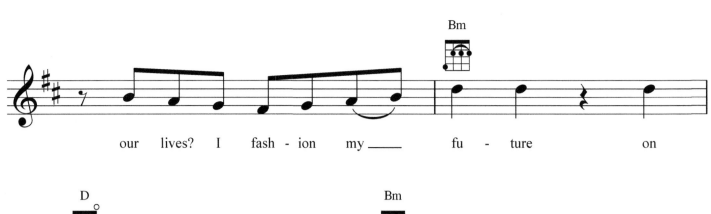

our lives? I fash - ion my _____ fu - ture on

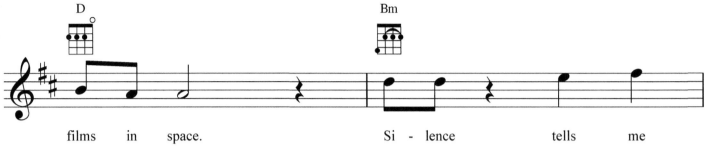

films in space. Si - lence tells me

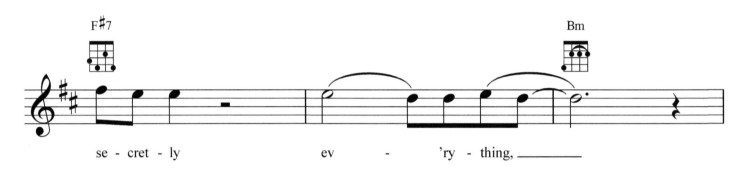

se - cret - ly ev - 'ry - thing, _____

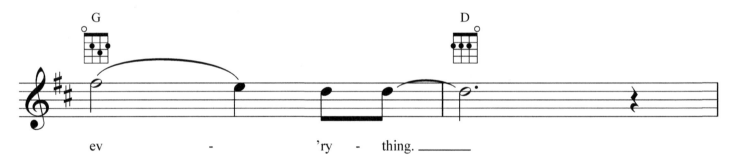

ev - 'ry - thing. _____

D.C. al Coda

Coda

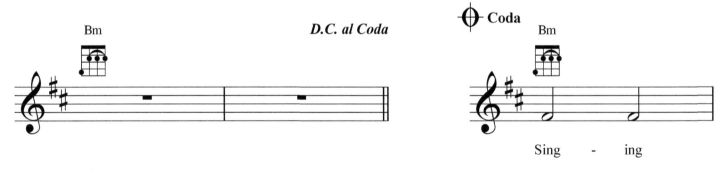

Sing - ing

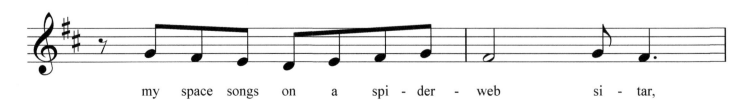

my space songs on a spi - der - web si - tar,

"Life is a - round ___ you and in you."

An - swer for Tim - o - thy ___ Lear - y,

Chorus

dear - y. ___ Let the sun ___

___ shine, ___ let the sun ___

___ shine in, ___ the sun ___ shine

1. – 4.

in.

5.

in.

Over the Rainbow

Music by Harold Arlen
Lyric by E.Y. "Yip" Harburg

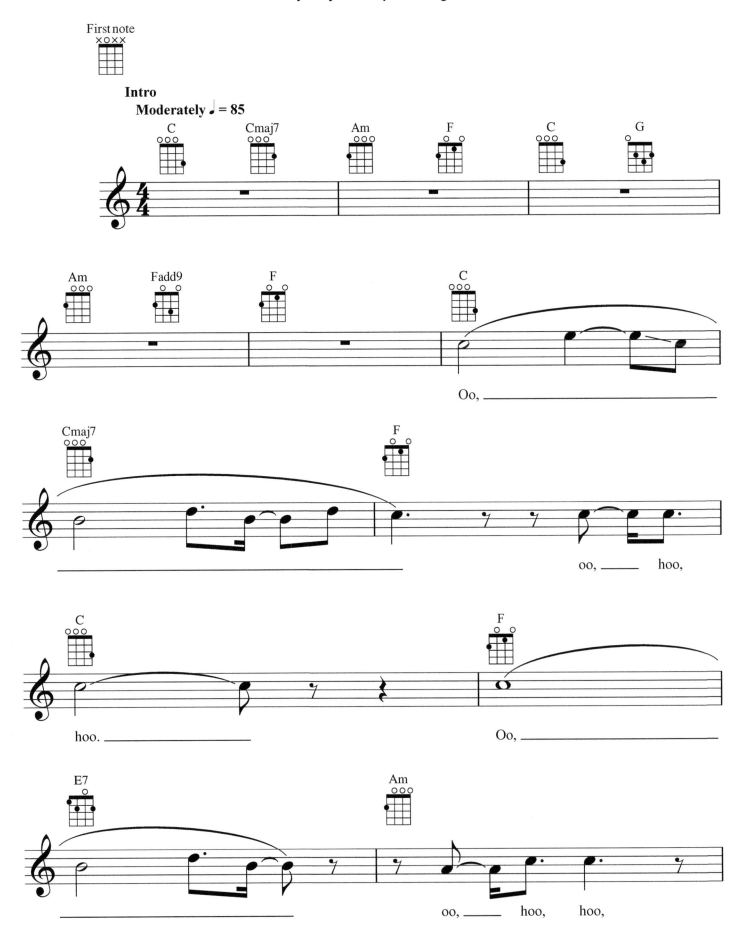

Verse

3., 4. Some - where o - ver ___ the rain - bow, ___

{ blue - birds fly. }
{ way ___ up high. }

And the

dreams that ___ you dare to. ___ Oh why, oh why can't

To Coda

Tip-Toe Thru' the Tulips with Me

Words by Al Dubin
Music by Joe Burke

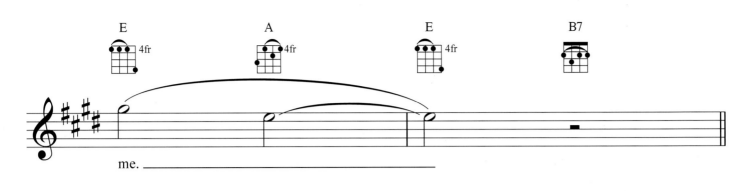

me. _____

Interlude

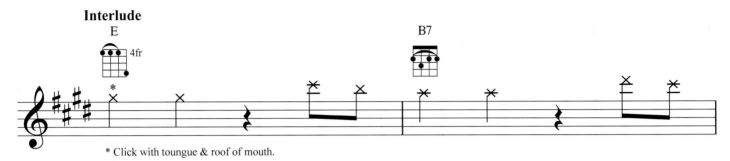

* Click with toungue & roof of mouth.

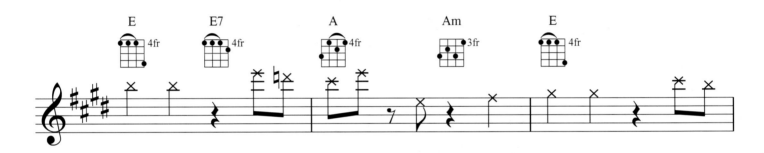

D.S. al Coda

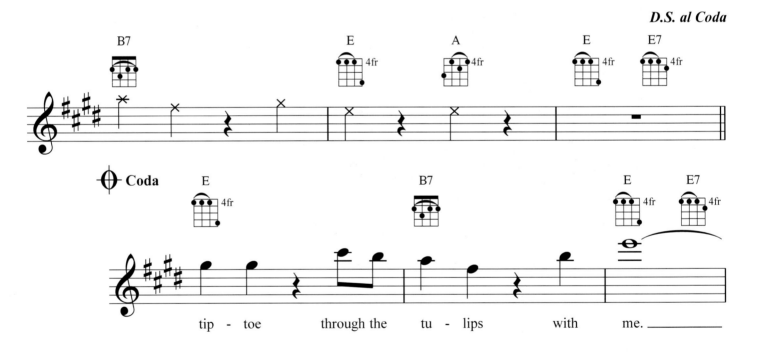

Coda

tip - toe   through the   tu - lips   with   me. _____

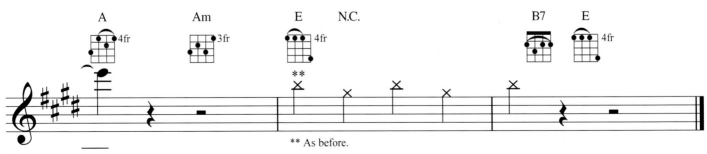

_____   ** As before.